PIANO . VOCAL . GUITAR

CORY CHISEL
AND THE WANDERING SONS
DEATH WON'T SEND A LETTER

ISBN 978-1-4234-9171-2

7777 W. BLUEMOUND RD. P.O. BOX 13819 MILWAUKEE, WI 53213

In Australia Contact:
Hal Leonard Australia Pty. Ltd.
4 Lentara Court
Cheltenham, Victoria, 3192 Australia
Email: ausadmin@halleonard.com.au

For all works contained herein:
Unauthorized copying, arranging, adapting, recording, Internet posting, public performance,
or other distribution of the printed music in this publication is an infringement of copyright.
Infringers are liable under the law.

Visit Hal Leonard Online at
www.halleonard.com

4
BORN AGAIN

12
CALM DOWN

19
LONGER TIME AT SEA

26
ANGEL OF MINE

31
MY HEART WOULD BE THERE

36
CURIOUS THING

46
SO WRONG FOR ME

51
WHAT DO YOU NEED

59
LOVE IS GONE

64
TENNESSEE

71
MOCKINGBIRD

BORN AGAIN

Words and Music by CORY CHISEL,
ADRIEL HARRIS and BRENDAN BENSON

Moderately fast

Copyright © 2009 Sony/ATV Music Publishing LLC, Elanors Publishing, Chrysalis Music and Gladsad Music
All Rights on behalf of Sony/ATV Music Publishing LLC Administered by Sony/ATV Music Publishing LLC, 8 Music Square West, Nashville, TN 37203
All Rights on behalf of Gladsad Music Administered by Chrysalis Music
International Copyright Secured   All Rights Reserved

LONGER TIME AT SEA

Words and Music by
CORY CHISEL

* Recorded a half step higher.

Copyright © 2009 Sony/ATV Music Publishing LLC
All Rights Administered by Sony/ATV Music Publishing LLC, 8 Music Square West, Nashville, TN 37203
International Copyright Secured All Rights Reserved

ANGEL OF MINE

Words and Music by
CORY CHISEL

Copyright © 2009 Sony/ATV Music Publishing LLC
All Rights Administered by Sony/ATV Music Publishing LLC, 8 Music Square West, Nashville, TN 37203
International Copyright Secured   All Rights Reserved

Was I ___ born luck-y.

Al-ways a cur-i-ous thing ___ to be haunt-ed, my friend. Take what you can.

No love must die. There no tears ___ in your eyes ___ I ___

sup - pose, I sup - pose.

Oh, my dear friend,

please don't be care - less with time.

You're reach-ing in. You won't last this time.

I won't seek to see. To hell with your

char-i-ty. Not when I've got

eyes to see.

Al - ways a cur - i - ous thing to be hat - ed.

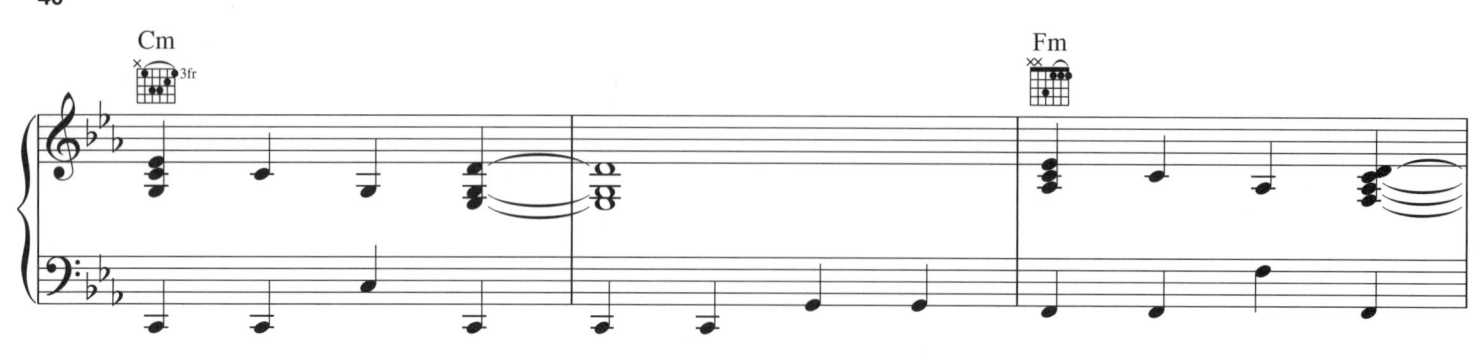

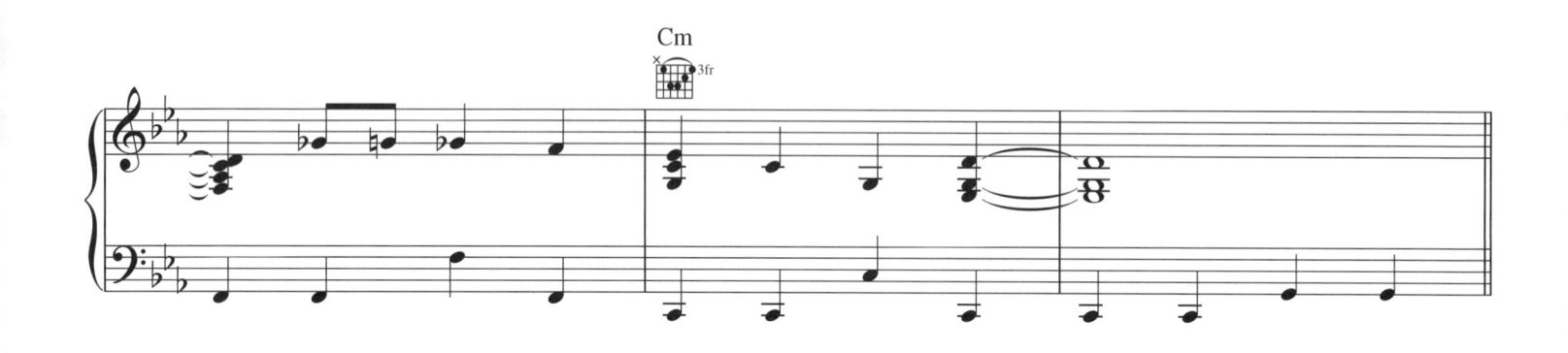

Oh, what a hor - ri - ble mark it can leave

on your skin.

see.

You know my mind.

It's not such a cur-ious

thing.

I guess I'll be fine.

Oh, my dear friend, please don't be care-less with time.

If you're reach-ing in, you won't

last this time. I won't seek to see.

I'm tired of your char-i-ty.

I've got eyes that see.

You know my mind.

You know my mind.

It's such a cur-i-ous thing.

I guess I'll be fine.

It's such a curious thing.

Repeat and Fade

SO WRONG FOR ME

Words and Music by
CORY CHISEL

Moderately fast

Oh, we've wad-ed out _____ a - cross the boil-ing o - cean waves. Mis-

Copyright © 2008 Chisel Publishing
All Rights Administered by Wixen Music Publishing, Inc.
International Copyright Secured   All Rights Reserved

takes were made. Your love is so wrong for me.____ Oh, well I just keep___ on try-in' to tear out my dreams.____
to pull the pen from the page,____

Nobody knows what nobody sees.
to pull the words from my mouth in a cold fit of rage.

I see this way to ru-in
But re-mem-ber me

sweet-ly and I see this way to grace.
in the dark of mid-

day.   Well, I just can't
But I've nev-er

E♭
3fr
B♭
Cm
3fr
A♭
4fr
stand to see a smile on your face if you thought for a min -
spoke to your skin in such a way. I just loved what I
E♭
3fr
B♭
Cm
3fr
ute I'd gone the right way.
can and I threw it a - way.
To Coda
My
A♭
4fr
E♭
3fr
dis-course lay dy - in' from the

life I've left un-done. Well, now

look what I've be-come.___ Your love is

D.S. al Coda

CODA

Your love is so wrong for me.___

Oh, but I just keep_ on try - in'.___

WHAT DO YOU NEED

Words and Music by
CORY CHISEL

Moderately fast

All my friends say they're not the fool, they say I'm the fool.
All the laugh-ter that was pour-in' out's just not com-in' now.

And all my lov-ers they don't
And all the hours spent

Copyright © 2009 Sony/ATV Music Publishing LLC
All Rights Administered by Sony/ATV Music Publishing LLC, 8 Music Square West, Nashville, TN 37203
International Copyright Secured   All Rights Reserved

un - der - stand __ what I ev - er need - ed you __ for, that I
pull - in' teeth __ just __ to keep you bus - y. It __

need - ed you __ for me. __
keeps me bus - y, too. __

They don't un - der - stand an - y -
thing a - bout __ me. They don't un - der - stand what it is a - bout __ me they

love.

And tell me what do you ___ need, ___ tell me what do you ___ need ___ from ___ me?

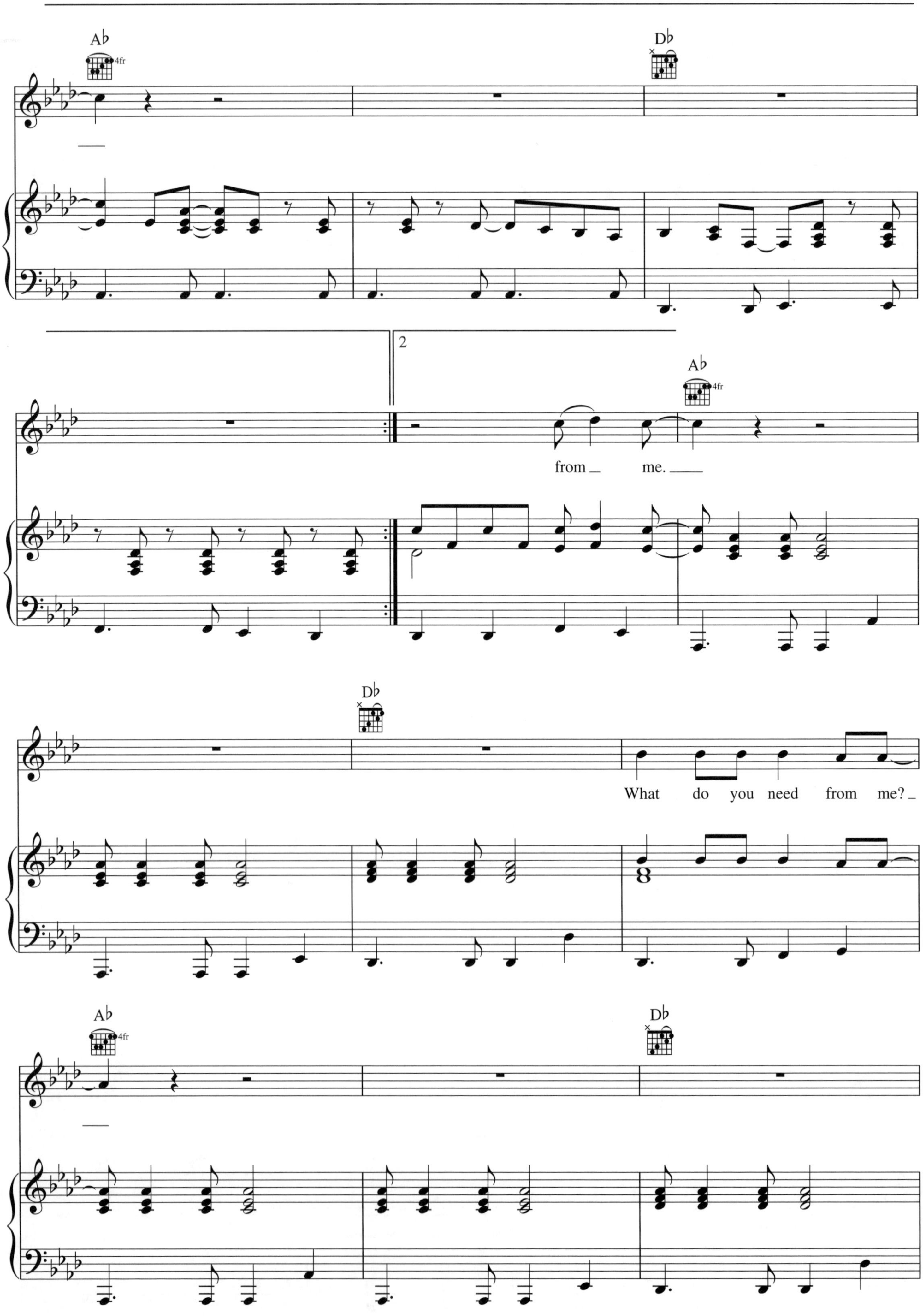
A♭
4fr
D♭
2
A♭
4fr
from _ me. ____
D♭
What do you need from me? _
A♭
4fr
D♭

What do you need from me? ___ 'Cause I'll be your Hou-di-ni.

I'll be your Hou-di-ni. ___ But you keep your pock-ets, you keep your pock-ets sewn.

A♭
4fr
You keep your pock - ets, you keep your pock - ets
B♭m
A♭
4fr
sewn. You keep your pock - ets sewn.
D♭
And tell me what do you
B♭m
D♭
need, tell me what

do you ____ need, ____ and tell me what ____ do you ____ need ____ from me?

Tell me what do you need from me?

What do you need from me?

What do you need from me?

LOVE IS GONE

Words and Music by
CORY CHISEL

Moderately

All of our love is gone. I see it clearly now. We're not the best of friends, but I'll still be in your crowd. Cut me with your song, oh, but don't

Copyright © 2009 Sony/ATV Music Publishing LLC
All Rights Administered by Sony/ATV Music Publishing LLC, 8 Music Square West, Nashville, TN 37203
International Copyright Secured   All Rights Reserved

___ let me bleed___ too long. ___

All of our love is gone. I saw it come and gone.
Our time has come and gone. I see it clear-ly now.
All of our love is gone. I feel it com-in' on.

I've been through man-y things and I can't for-get them all.
We're not the best of friends, but I'll still be in your crowd.
We've been through man-y things and I know I've done you wrong.

To Coda

(1.) How___ I do re-call when there's no-bod-y left___ in line?___
(2., D.S.) Cut___ me with your song, oh, but don't___ let me bleed___ too long.___

B♭m
B♭m(maj7)
6fr
B♭m7
E♭
3fr
B♭m
B♭m(maj7)
6fr
D.S. al Coda
B♭m7
E♭
3fr
A♭
4fr
CODA
B♭m
G♭
Cut me with your
D♭
F7
B♭m
song, but don't let me bleed.

Don't let me bleed too long.

Da da da da da da da da da da da

da da da da da da. Da da da da da da da

da da da da da da da da da da da. Da da da

da da da da da da da da da da da da da.

Da da da da da da da da da.

TENNESSEE

Words and Music by
CORY CHISEL

Moderately

Just swing a-cross the south-ern sky, lift a match to my morn-in' eyes. Well, we'll all die young if we're luck-y, babe.

Cast your light in-to my room. Kiss me deep-er, I'm leav-in' soon. We're far too young to be dy-in' now.

Copyright © 2009 Sony/ATV Music Publishing LLC
All Rights Administered by Sony/ATV Music Publishing LLC, 8 Music Square West, Nashville, TN 37203
International Copyright Secured All Rights Reserved

You'd / Just

hate the dark to prove the dawn. Need me no more and
draw me down with ev-'ry word till we find out

I'll be gone. I'm dy'n' to love some-
we de-serve I know I can-not

bod-y like you loved him. And you
pay my debt-or's fee. But you

look just like dar - lin' Ten - nes - see. Do you think she'll know or see me now like the broken man I am? Doin' a little bit more than the best I can. Still she's gon - na need a lit - tle more.

So I would

stand in __ dis - grace.

I would spit in __ my sav - ior's __ face, __

my coat tat - tered __ and torn,

just to know that my love will be re - born.

And our days pass like Au - tumn wind.

And the world spins a - round me a - gain. And you look just like my dar- lin' Ten- nes- see.

Well, we'll all die young if we're luck- y, babe.

MOCKINGBIRD

Words and Music by
CORY CHISEL

Moderately fast

Wel-come to the warmth, my dear son from the North. You look bet-ter these days than you did. Your speak-ing is slow, and I'll let you know but you're suf-f'ring each stroke of your heart. Tell me

Copyright © 2009 Sony/ATV Music Publishing LLC
All Rights Administered by Sony/ATV Music Publishing LLC, 8 Music Square West, Nashville, TN 37203
International Copyright Secured   All Rights Reserved

when did your life come a-part.

With your writ-ings re-cit-ed, the jur-y's de-cid-ed that your ex-ile has been self-in-duced. With your proph-e-cies tram-pled, your poor heart un-rav-eled, searched out for some strand of truth.

And love is a game to be played on a Mock-ing-bird stage. And I would have you for my own. Two heels kick like steel drums on a tiled kit-chen floor. Do not ask my for-give-ness, not when you still need more. Like a watch-man in the tower, I've seen you bloom like a flower. But you are fad-ing in the ab-sence of rain. And your love is a game to be played on a Mock-ing-bird stage.

Dm
Gm
3fr
A
And I would have you for my
Dm
3
own.
And there'll come a time when we all,
A+/C♯
2fr
G
Dm
all must stand be - fore we fall.
Gm
3fr
A
Dm
To Coda
And I'm gon-na be there when you do.

So pour out for your spec-ta-tors dreams and in-ten-tions, still nothing is sweet-er de-spite all your in-ven-tions. And the few se-cret prom-is-es locked in your rhyme, my love, noth-ing is chang-ing with time. You're just los-ing your pre-cious mind.

D.S. al Coda
CODA
And your love is a
So,
A+/C♯
Gm
cry like _ Saint Chris-to-pher, or preach like _ Saint Paul. Still your lips they're _ for it, and they're
Dm
B♭
no help _ at all. 'Cause you can't sue _ the li - ons, no, you
F
E♭
Dm
can't raise _ the dead. You are John the Bap - tist and they are tak - ing your head.